Be Still

Women Living Well

3-MONTH HABIT TRACKER

Start Date

Be Still: Women Living Well 3-Month Habit Tracker

Cover and interior layout and design by Five J's Design
Cover image credit: Karma (Adobe Stock)

Table of Contents

Do you feel like there are **not enough hours in the day?**

Do you make goals and then **have trouble reaching them?**

Do you feel like **important priorities get pushed aside** because of the tyranny of the urgent?

YOU ARE NOT ALONE. All of us struggle to stay disciplined day in and day out. For a Christian, setting aside time to be alone with God helps us to make wise choices with our time. How will we know how to spend our time—what we should commit to and what we should say "no" to, if we are not in communion with God? Without God's guidance, most likely we will take on more than we ought.

Jesus says, "Come to me, all you who are weary and burdened, and I will give you rest.
29 Take my yoke upon you and learn from me, for I am gentle and humble in heart, and you will find rest for your souls." (Matthew 11:28,29)

When our stress levels are high—it is nearly impossible to be the person we want to be. It is difficult to be self-controlled. We are too busy and there is absolutely no room for error in the day. We all need room to breathe. We need time to hear from God in his word. We need time to read a mind stretching and soul-inspiring book or to soak in a bubble bath or to journal or to linger long with loved ones. These are gifts that God has given us to enjoy.

What gifts are you missing out on because you are lacking self-discipline in your life?

I hope this Habit Tracker will be a secret weapon to helping you reach your personal goals. It will help you track your progress and build discipline into your daily life. But beware – do not try to complete all the trackers at once! Pick and choose the ones that fit your personal goals. Then attempt to complete those few trackers. Do not be discouraged. No one can do it all. Be wise in your choices. Pray and ask the Lord to show you which of these trackers will grow your mind, body or soul and then get started!

You are not alone on your journey! Join me on the blog at **WomenLivingWell.org** and out on Instagram at **Instagram.com/WomenLivingWell**

Together we can reach our goals.

Walk with the King,

Courtney

"For God
gave us a spirit not of fear
but of power and love
and self-control."

2 TIMOTHY 1:7

How to Use the Trackers

This 3-month tracker was designed to help you reach your life goals. Each of us has a unique set of priorities, but all of us should be growing in our walk with the Lord.

Instructions for how to use each individual tracker can be found on the following pages, but first, here's how everything is organized.

- The first thing you'll find (on p. 21) is a place to track your **Prayer Requests and Bible Reading.** These spiritual trackers are to be used for all three months.
- Behind the spiritual trackers (on p. 29), you will find **three sets of seven Habit Trackers** separated by month. When the book is closed, you can easily find the month you want by looking at the black tabs on the edges of the pages. The seven trackers that are included in each of the three monthly sections are:
    1. a Health Tracker
    2. a Sleep Tracker
    3. a Calorie Tracker
    4. a Housework Tracker
    5. a Meal Planning Tracker
    6. a Gratitude Tracker
    7. a Note Tracker
- Behind the three months of Habit Trackers (on p. 83), you will find **90 lined pages for journaling**, along with an inspirational verse every other day.

The more often you complete a habit, the stronger the habit will become. As you track your success and identify areas of weakness, you will find motivation to keep your good habits going.

Enjoy the journey of growth and progress, and remember to give yourself grace as you live intentionally, to the glory of God!

HOW TO USE THE

Prayer Request Tracker

Have you ever told someone you would pray for them—and then you forgot? Using this prayer tracker will remind you to pray and to follow up and watch for answered prayers. When a prayer is answered, highlight it or date the day it was answered.

There are three pages provided for you to log your prayer requests. If you run out of space, flip to the back of your book and use the journal pages to continue your prayer requests.

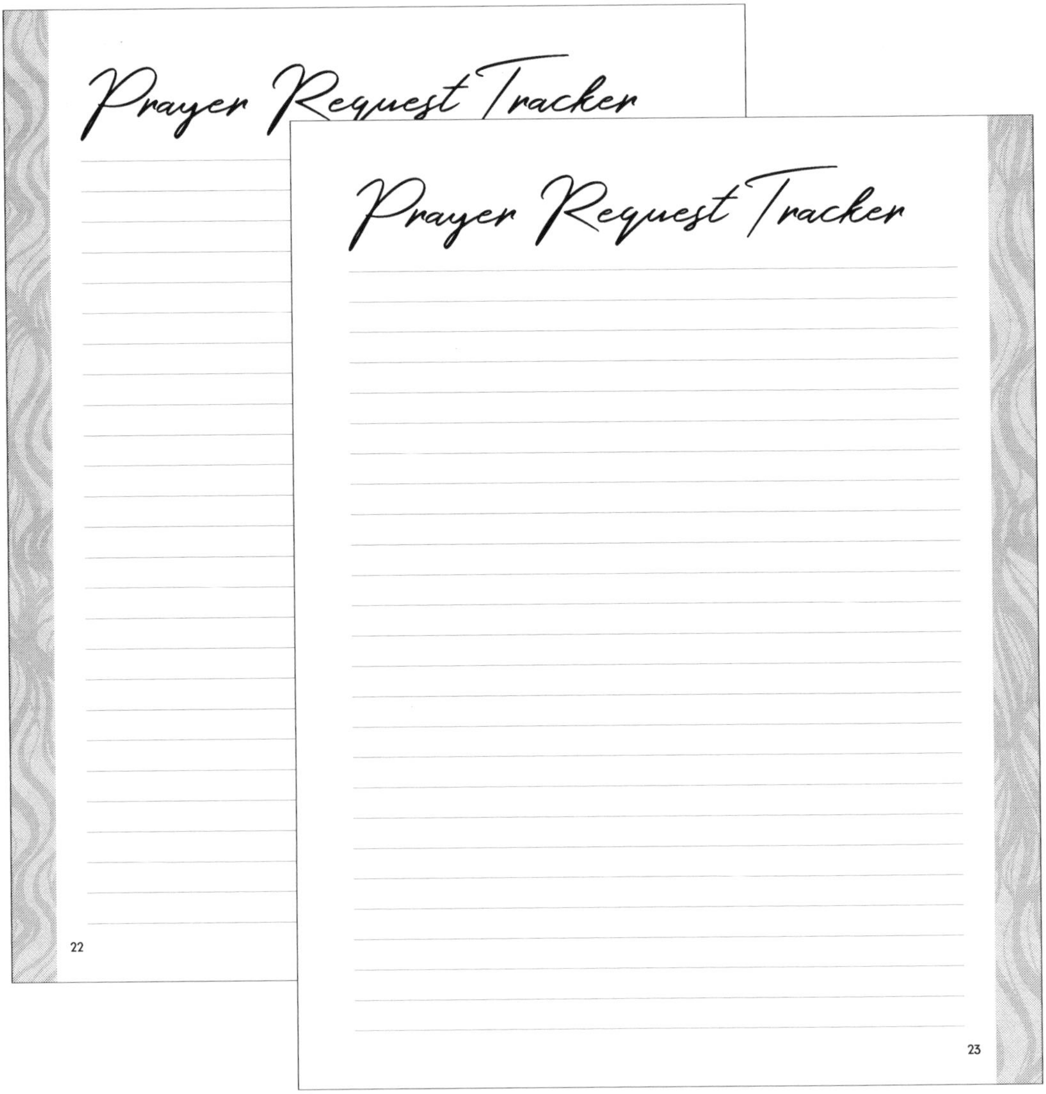

Prayer Request Tracker

22

Prayer Request Tracker

23

HOW TO USE THE

Proverbs Tracker

Do you need more wisdom and insight for your daily life? Then Proverbs is a great book of the Bible for you to read. Read one chapter a day and use the Proverbs Tracker to track your reading.

Proverbs Tracker

Month 1			Month 2			Month 3		
DAY OF THE MONTH	CHAPTER	✔	DAY OF THE MONTH	CHAPTER	✔	DAY OF THE MONTH	CHAPTER	✔
1	Proverbs 1		1	Proverbs 1		1	Proverbs 1	
2	Proverbs 2		2	Proverbs 2		2	Proverbs 2	
3	Proverbs 3		3	Proverbs 3		3	Proverbs 3	
4	Proverbs 4		4	Proverbs 4		4	Proverbs 4	
5	Proverbs 5		5	Proverbs 5		5	Proverbs 5	
6	Proverbs 6		6	Proverbs 6		6	Proverbs 6	
7	Proverbs 7		7	Proverbs 7		7	Proverbs 7	
8	Proverbs 8		8	Proverbs 8		8	Proverbs 8	
9	Proverbs 9		9	Proverbs 9		9	Proverbs 9	
10	Proverbs 10		10	Proverbs 10		10	Proverbs 10	
11	Proverbs 11		11	Proverbs 11		11	Proverbs 11	
12	Proverbs 12		12	Proverbs 12		12	Proverbs 12	
13	Proverbs 13		13	Proverbs 13		13	Proverbs 13	
14	Proverbs 14		14	Proverbs 14		14	Proverbs 14	
15	Proverbs 15		15	Proverbs 15		15	Proverbs 15	
16	Proverbs 16		16	Proverbs 16		16	Proverbs 16	
17	Proverbs 17		17	Proverbs 17		17	Proverbs 17	
18	Proverbs 18		18	Proverbs 18		18	Proverbs 18	
19	Proverbs 19		19	Proverbs 19		19	Proverbs 19	
20	Proverbs 20		20	Proverbs 20		20	Proverbs 20	
21	Proverbs 21		21	Proverbs 21		21	Proverbs 21	
22	Proverbs 22		22	Proverbs 22		22	Proverbs 22	
23	Proverbs 23		23	Proverbs 23		23	Proverbs 23	
24	Proverbs 24		24	Proverbs 24		24	Proverbs 24	
25	Proverbs 25		25	Proverbs 25		25	Proverbs 25	
26	Proverbs 26		26	Proverbs 26		26	Proverbs 26	
27	Proverbs 27		27	Proverbs 27		27	Proverbs 27	
28	Proverbs 28		28	Proverbs 28		28	Proverbs 28	
29	Proverbs 29		29	Proverbs 29		29	Proverbs 29	
30	Proverbs 30		30	Proverbs 30		30	Proverbs 30	
31	Proverbs 31		31	Proverbs 31		31	Proverbs 31	

25

HOW TO USE THE

Old & New Testament Tracker

Have you felt frustrated when you've fallen behind on a "Read Through the Bible in a Year" plan? Me too! So many times the dates on the plan lead me to feel like a failure. But this tracker has no dates! Simply pick any book of the Bible and begin reading a chapter—or two or three—each day. Log your progress, and enjoy the grace this tracker offers you.

Old Testam

GENESIS 1 2 3 4 5 6 7 8 9 10 11 12 13 14 15 16 17 18 19 20 21 22 23 24 25 26 27 28 29 30 31 32 33 34 35 36 37 38 39 40 41 42 43 44 45 46 47 48 49 50

EXODUS 1 2 3 4 5 6 7 8 9 10 11 12 13 14 15 16 17 18 19 20 21 22 23 24 25 26 27 28 29 30 31 32 33 34 35 36 37 38 39 40

LEVITICUS 1 2 3 4 5 6 7 8 9 10 11 12 13 14 15 16 17 18 19 20 21 22 23 24 25 26 27

NUMBERS 1 2 3 4 5 6 7 8 9 10 11 12 13 14 15 16 17 18 19 20 21 22 23 24 25 26 27 28 29 30 31 32 33 34 35 36

DEUTERONOMY 1 2 3 4 5 6 7 8 9 10 11 12 13 14 15 16 17 18 19 20 21 22 23 24 25 26 27 28 29 30 31 32 33 34

JOSHUA 1 2 3 4 5 6 7 8 9 10 11 12 13 14 15 16 17 18 19 20 21 22 23 24

JUDGES 1 2 3 4 5 6 7 8 9 10 11 12 13 14 15 16 17 18 19 20 21

RUTH 1 2 3 4

1 SAMUEL 8 9 10 18 19 20 28 29 30

2 SAMUEL 8 9 10 18 19 20

1 KINGS 8 9 10 18 19 20

2 KINGS 8 9 10 18 19 20

1 CHRONIC 7 8 9 17 18 19 27 28 29

2 CHRONIC 7 8 9 17 18 19 27 28 29

EZRA 1 2 3

NEHEMIAH 8 9 10

ESTHER 1 2 3

26

JEREMIAH 1 2 3 4 5 6 7 8 9 10 11 12 13 14 15 16 17 18 19 20 21 22 23 24 25 26 27 28 29 30 31 32 33 34 35 36 37 38 39 40 41 42 43 44 45 46 47 48 49 50 51 52

LAMENTATIONS 1 2 3 4 5

EZEKIEL 1 2 3 4 5 6 7 8 9 10 11 12 13 14 15 16 17 18 19 20 21 22 23 24 25 26 27 28 29 30 31 32 33 34 35 36 37 38 39 40 41 42 43 44 45 46 47 48

DANIEL 1 2 3 4 5 6 7 8 9 10 11 12

HOSEA 1 2 3 4 5 6 7 8 9 10 11 12 13 14

JOEL 1 2 3

AMOS 1 2 3 4 5 6 7 8 9

OBADIAH 1

JONAH 1 2 3 4

MICAH 1 2 3 4 5 6 7

NAHUM 1 2 3

HABAKKUK 1 2 3

ZEPHANIAH 1 2 3

HAGGAI 1 2

ZECHARIAH 1 2 3 4 5 6 7 8 9 10 11 12 13 14

MALACHI 1 2 3 4

New Testament

MATTHEW 1 2 3 4 5 6 7 8 9 10 11 12 13 14 15 16 17 18 19 20 21 22 23 24 25 26 27 28

MARK 1 2 3 4 5 6 7 8 9 10 11 12 13 14 15 16

LUKE 1 2 3 4 5 6 7 8 9 10 11 12 13 14 15 16 17 18 19 20 21 22 23 24

JOHN 1 2 3 4 5 6 7 8 9 10 11 12 13 14 15 16 17 18 19 20 21

ACTS 1 2 3 4 5 6 7 8 9 10 11 12 13 14 15 16 17 18 19 20 21 22 23 24 25 26 27 28

ROMANS 1 2 3 4 5 6 7 8 9 10 11 12 13 14 15 16

1 CORINTHIANS 1 2 3 4 5 6 7 8 9 10 11 12 13 14 15 16

2 CORINTHIANS 1 2 3 4 5 6 7 8 9 10 11 12 13

GALATIANS 1 2 3 4 5 6

EPHESIANS 1 2 3 4 5 6

PHILIPPIANS 1 2 3 4

COLOSSIANS 1 2 3 4

1 THESSALONIANS 1 2 3 4 5

2 THESSALONIANS 1 2 3

1 TIMOTHY 1 2 3 4 5 6

2 TIMOTHY 1 2 3 4

TITUS 1 2 3

PHILEMON 1

HEBREWS 1 2 3 4 5 6 7 8 9 10 11 12 13

JAMES 1 2 3 4 5

1 PETER 1 2 3 4 5

2 PETER 1 2 3

1 JOHN 1 2 3 4 5

2 JOHN 1

3 JOHN 1

JUDE 1

REVELATION 1 2 3 4 5 6 7 8 9 10 11 12 13 14 15 16 17 18 19 20 21 22

27

HOW TO USE THE

Health Tracker

Do you have workout equipment that you spent a lot of money on but rarely use? Making goals and tracking our progress helps us to be more mindful and conscious of our daily choices. Use this Health Tracker to create your own personal health goals. For example, determine how many minutes of cardio or strength training you want to complete each day. If there are some days you want to take off, color those squares in. Then on the other days, track your progress. Create personal goals regarding your fruit and vegetable intake or limiting the time you spend on social media. If there is an item on the tracker you do not want to track, strike out that row with a black marker. If there is an item missing from the tracker, use the blank rows to add in what you would like to track.

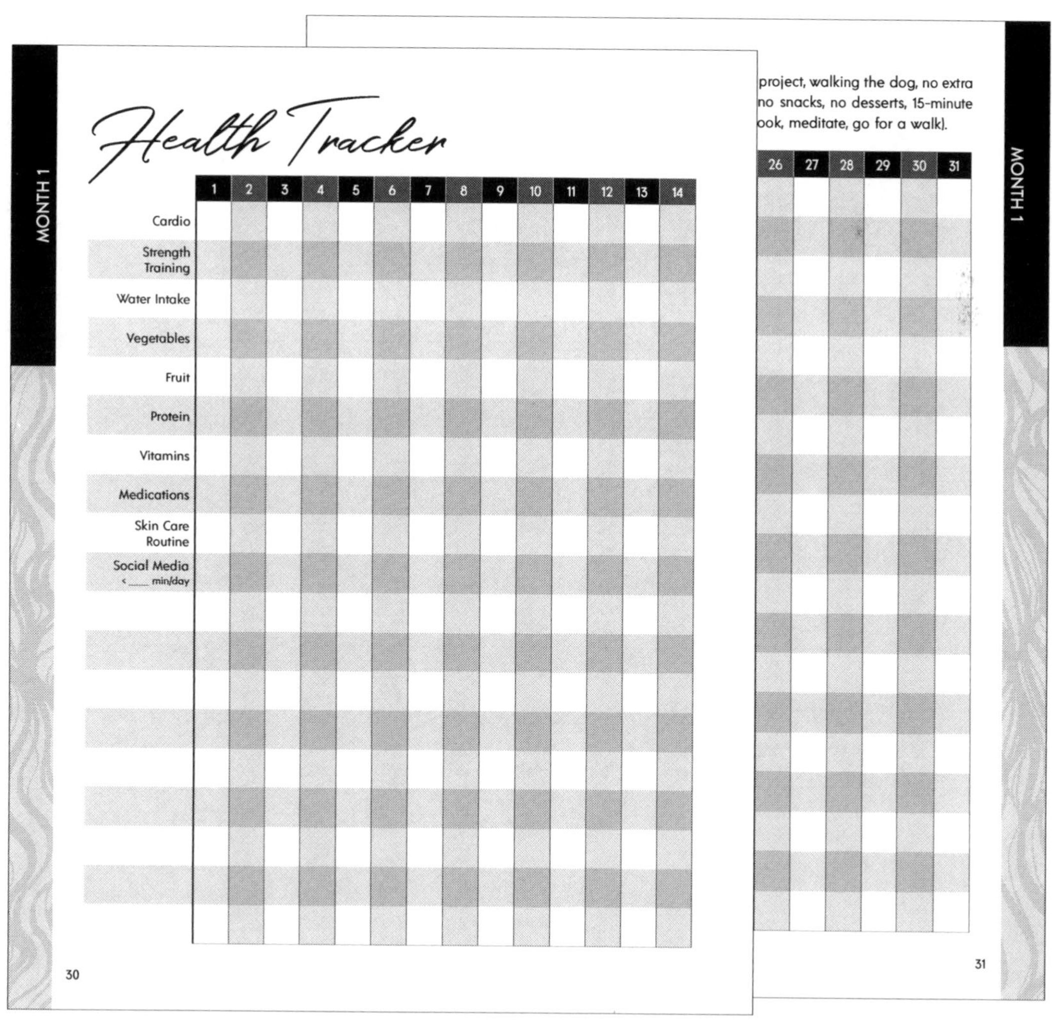

HOW TO USE THE

Sleep Tracker

Did you know that we will spend almost one-third of our lives sleeping? Poor sleep can lead to poor health. Sleep is vital for longevity; God created our bodies to require rest. But many of us are short on sleep, and it is affecting our daily lives. Color in the boxes of the hours you sleep on the tracker to track your sleep each night along with any naps you take.

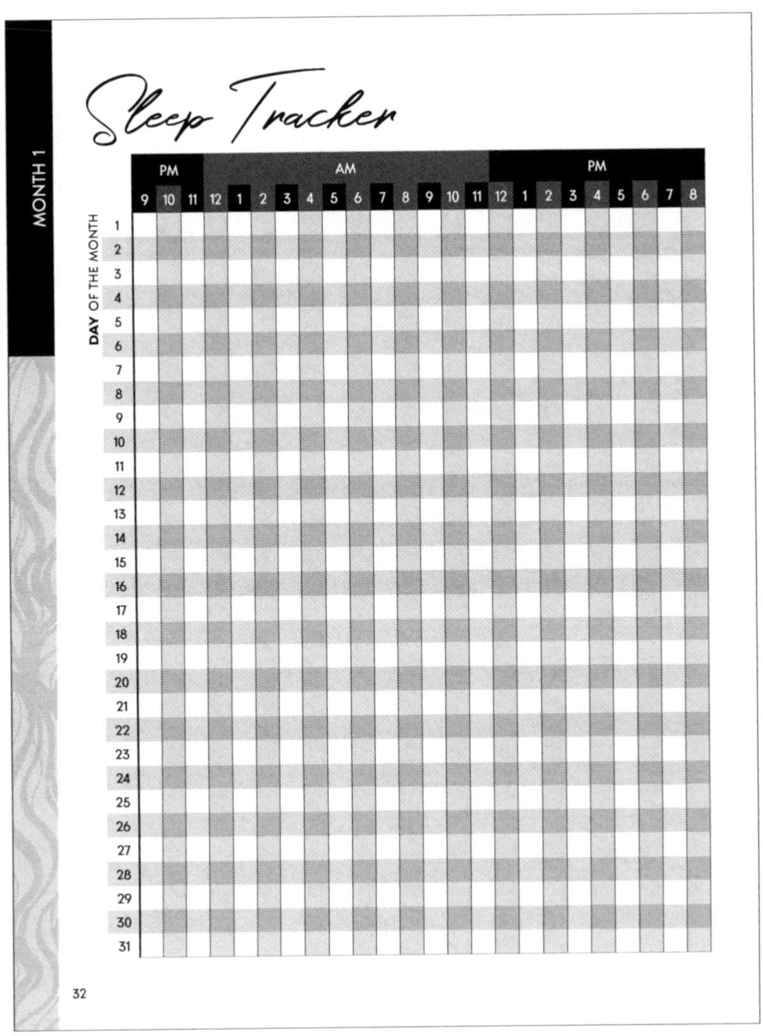

MONTH 1

Sleep Tracker

DAY OF THE MONTH	PM			AM												PM								
	9	10	11	12	1	2	3	4	5	6	7	8	9	10	11	12	1	2	3	4	5	6	7	8
1																								
2																								
3																								
4																								
5																								
6																								
7																								
8																								
9																								
10																								
11																								
12																								
13																								
14																								
15																								
16																								
17																								
18																								
19																								
20																								
21																								
22																								
23																								
24																								
25																								
26																								
27																								
28																								
29																								
30																								
31																								

32

HOW TO USE THE

Calorie Tracker

Do you need to watch your calorie intake? Counting calories is not for everyone, so some may wish to skip this tracker altogether. But if you fall into the percentage of women who do track their calories from time to time, this is for you. The number of calories each of us needs in a day varies, so choose your number and then begin logging as you eat each meal. If you need a tool to help you determine the number of calories in the foods you eat, **MyFitnessPal.com** offers a free online calorie counter.

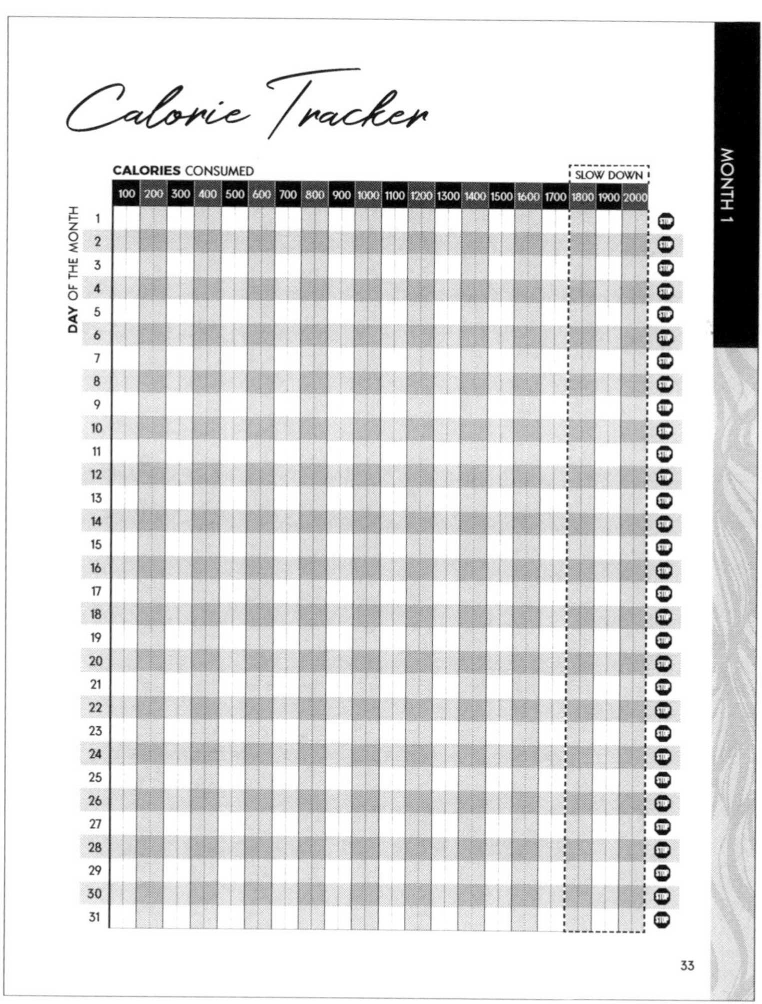

Calorie Tracker

MONTH 1

CALORIES CONSUMED

SLOW DOWN

DAY OF THE MONTH	100	200	300	400	500	600	700	800	900	1000	1100	1200	1300	1400	1500	1600	1700	1800	1900	2000	
1																					STOP
2																					STOP
3																					STOP
4																					STOP
5																					STOP
6																					STOP
7																					STOP
8																					STOP
9																					STOP
10																					STOP
11																					STOP
12																					STOP
13																					STOP
14																					STOP
15																					STOP
16																					STOP
17																					STOP
18																					STOP
19																					STOP
20																					STOP
21																					STOP
22																					STOP
23																					STOP
24																					STOP
25																					STOP
26																					STOP
27																					STOP
28																					STOP
29																					STOP
30																					STOP
31																					STOP

33

HOW TO USE THE

Housework Tracker

Do you struggle to get all of your housework done? Routines and habits work to get the job done. Create your own unique weekly routine and then implement it using the Housework Tracker. Common weekly chores are listed for you. Use the blanks to add in other chores that may be on your personal list like ironing, cleaning out the refrigerator, or organizing a closet.

MONTH 1

Housework Tracker

	WEEK 1							WEEK 2							WEEK 3							WEEK 4							WEEK 5						
	S	M	T	W	T	F	S	S	M	T	W	T	F	S	S	M	T	W	T	F	S	S	M	T	W	T	F	S	S	M	T	W	T	F	S
Menu Plan																																			
Grocery Shop																																			
Wash Laundry																																			
Fold Laundry																																			
Put Away Laundry																																			
Dust																																			
Vacuum/Sweep																																			
Empty Trash Cans																																			
Clean Bathrooms																																			
Clean Kitchen																																			

	SUNDAY	MONDAY	TUESDAY	WEDNESDAY	THURSDAY	FRIDAY	SATURDAY
SUGGESTED ROUTINE	REST!	market day	tubs, toilets & towels	wash day	dust & vacuum	floor	catch-up day

	SUNDAY	MONDAY	TUESDAY	WEDNESDAY	THURSDAY	FRIDAY	SATURDAY
MY WEEKLY ROUTINE							

	SUNDAY	MONDAY	TUESDAY	WEDNESDAY	THURSDAY	FRIDAY	SATURDAY
MY WEEKLY ROUTINE							

	SUNDAY	MONDAY	TUESDAY	WEDNESDAY	THURSDAY	FRIDAY	SATURDAY
MY WEEKLY ROUTINE							

	SUNDAY	MONDAY	TUESDAY	WEDNESDAY	THURSDAY	FRIDAY	SATURDAY
MY WEEKLY ROUTINE							

34

HOW TO USE THE

Meal Planning Tracker

Did you know you will eat over 1,000 meals in the next year? That's a lot to organize, especially if you have a lot of mouths to feed. Planning our meals ahead for the week or month can help us eat healthier, save money, get food on the table faster, and avoid that stressful feeling when we are scrambling to decide what to cook. Make your shopping list based on your meal plan. This way you'll be able to avoid last-minute shopping and have all the ingredients you need for the week. The more you meal plan, the easier those 1,000 meals become. There are five weeks of Meal Planning Trackers included in each month.

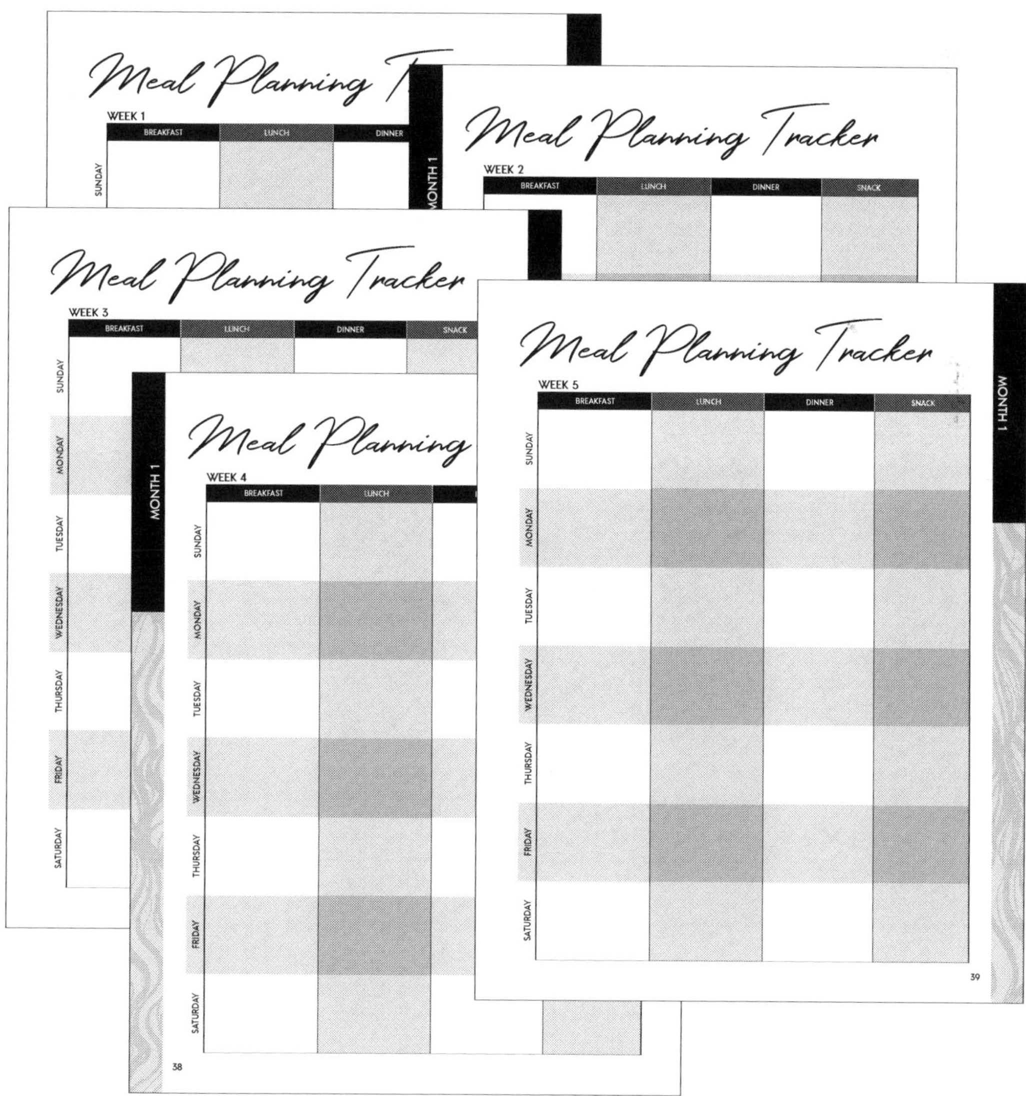

HOW TO USE THE *Gratitude Tracker*

Are you aware of all the benefits of a Gratitude Tracker? It is scientifically proven that listing the things we are grateful for improves our mood, our relationships, our physical and psychological health, our sleep, our hopefulness, and our resilience. Spiritually speaking, recognizing what we're grateful for opens our eyes to the good gifts that God has generously given to us each day. Write out the things that you're grateful for each day, and then use the section at the end of the Gratitude Tracker to write out your reflections on how tracking the things you are grateful for has impacted your life.

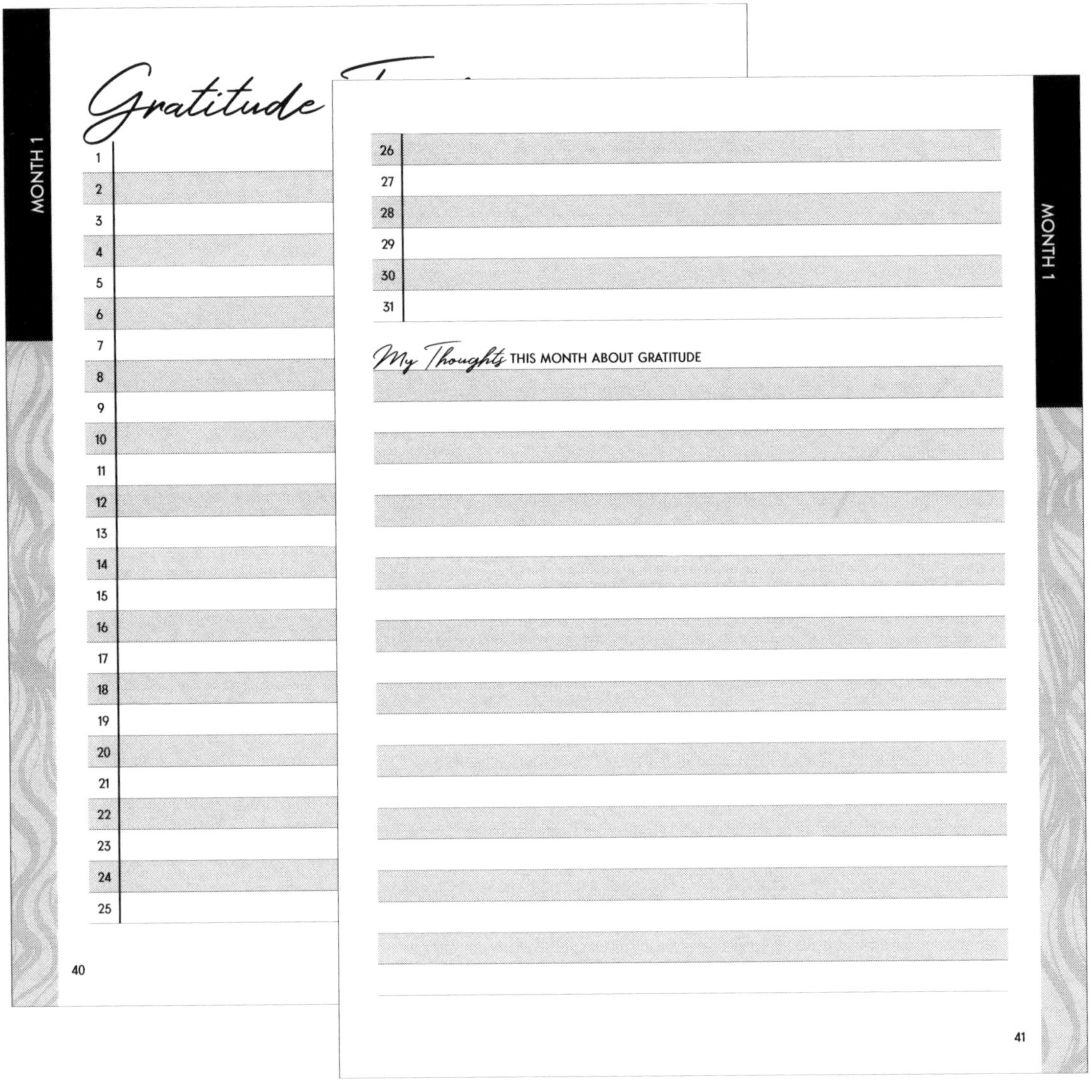

MONTH 1

Gratitude T

1
2
3
4
5
6
7
8
9
10
11
12
13
14
15
16
17
18
19
20
21
22
23
24
25

40

26
27
28
29
30
31

My Thoughts THIS MONTH ABOUT GRATITUDE

MONTH 1

41

HOW TO USE THE
Notes Tracker

Do you listen to podcasts or sermons on-line? We tend to remember the things we write down. Use this tracker to take notes about ideas and thoughts you either learned or do not want to forget. You could also use these pages to take notes in church while your pastor preaches. There are five Notes Trackers included in each month.

MONTH 1

Notes Tracker

TITLE: SPEAKER:

42

HOW TO USE THE

Journaling Pages

Did you know that journaling daily can increase self-awareness, release pent-up emotions, help us to focus, and lead to healing? Your journal can be used in various ways. You could use it to write out your prayers, Bible verses, take notes from your daily Bible reading or other books you are reading, write out your emotions and struggles, capture brilliant ideas, or write out your dreams and goals. You could sketch in it, journal your daily happenings, write unsent letters, store quotes, make to-do lists, keep recipes, log expenses, make buckets lists, and more! Whatever is on your mind, write it.

Journal

84

"But they who wait for the Lord shall renew their strength."
ISAIAH 40:31

85

A Final Note

It is not easy to do these Habit Trackers daily, but it is so good for us! Choose today to begin, and see where it leads. If you need extra accountability, invite a friend or a group of friends to work through these trackers together. Discuss your progress and cheer each other on. This is your journey to take. Enjoy it!

Prayer Requests & Bible Reading

Prayer Request Tracker

Prayer Request Tracker

Prayer Request Tracker

Proverbs Tracker

Month 1

DAY OF THE MONTH	CHAPTER	✔
1	Proverbs 1	
2	Proverbs 2	
3	Proverbs 3	
4	Proverbs 4	
5	Proverbs 5	
6	Proverbs 6	
7	Proverbs 7	
8	Proverbs 8	
9	Proverbs 9	
10	Proverbs 10	
11	Proverbs 11	
12	Proverbs 12	
13	Proverbs 13	
14	Proverbs 14	
15	Proverbs 15	
16	Proverbs 16	
17	Proverbs 17	
18	Proverbs 18	
19	Proverbs 19	
20	Proverbs 20	
21	Proverbs 21	
22	Proverbs 22	
23	Proverbs 23	
24	Proverbs 24	
25	Proverbs 25	
26	Proverbs 26	
27	Proverbs 27	
28	Proverbs 28	
29	Proverbs 29	
30	Proverbs 30	
31	Proverbs 31	

Month 2

DAY OF THE MONTH	CHAPTER	✔
1	Proverbs 1	
2	Proverbs 2	
3	Proverbs 3	
4	Proverbs 4	
5	Proverbs 5	
6	Proverbs 6	
7	Proverbs 7	
8	Proverbs 8	
9	Proverbs 9	
10	Proverbs 10	
11	Proverbs 11	
12	Proverbs 12	
13	Proverbs 13	
14	Proverbs 14	
15	Proverbs 15	
16	Proverbs 16	
17	Proverbs 17	
18	Proverbs 18	
19	Proverbs 19	
20	Proverbs 20	
21	Proverbs 21	
22	Proverbs 22	
23	Proverbs 23	
24	Proverbs 24	
25	Proverbs 25	
26	Proverbs 26	
27	Proverbs 27	
28	Proverbs 28	
29	Proverbs 29	
30	Proverbs 30	
31	Proverbs 31	

Month 3

DAY OF THE MONTH	CHAPTER	✔
1	Proverbs 1	
2	Proverbs 2	
3	Proverbs 3	
4	Proverbs 4	
5	Proverbs 5	
6	Proverbs 6	
7	Proverbs 7	
8	Proverbs 8	
9	Proverbs 9	
10	Proverbs 10	
11	Proverbs 11	
12	Proverbs 12	
13	Proverbs 13	
14	Proverbs 14	
15	Proverbs 15	
16	Proverbs 16	
17	Proverbs 17	
18	Proverbs 18	
19	Proverbs 19	
20	Proverbs 20	
21	Proverbs 21	
22	Proverbs 22	
23	Proverbs 23	
24	Proverbs 24	
25	Proverbs 25	
26	Proverbs 26	
27	Proverbs 27	
28	Proverbs 28	
29	Proverbs 29	
30	Proverbs 30	
31	Proverbs 31	

Old Testament

GENESIS

1	2	3	4	5	6	7	8	9	10
11	12	13	14	15	16	17	18	19	20
21	22	23	24	25	26	27	28	29	30
31	32	33	34	35	36	37	38	39	40
41	42	43	44	45	46	47	48	49	50

EXODUS

1	2	3	4	5	6	7	8	9	10
11	12	13	14	15	16	17	18	19	20
21	22	23	24	25	26	27	28	29	30
31	32	33	34	35	36	37	38	39	40

LEVITICUS

1	2	3	4	5	6	7	8	9	10
11	12	13	14	15	16	17	18	19	20
21	22	23	24	25	26	27			

NUMBERS

			1	2	3	4	5	6	7
8	9	10	11	12	13	14	15	16	17
18	19	20	21	22	23	24	25	26	27
28	29	30	31	32	33	34	35	36	

DEUTERONOMY

				1	2	3	4	5	6
7	8	9	10	11	12	13	14	15	16
17	18	19	20	21	22	23	24	25	26
27	28	29	30	31	32	33	34		

JOSHUA

			1	2	3	4	5	6	7
8	9	10	11	12	13	14	15	16	17
18	19	20	21	22	23	24			

JUDGES

			1	2	3	4	5	6	7
8	9	10	11	12	13	14	15	16	17
18	19	20	21						

RUTH

1	2	3	4

1 SAMUEL

			1	2	3	4	5	6	7
8	9	10	11	12	13	14	15	16	17
18	19	20	21	22	23	24	25	26	27
28	29	30	31						

2 SAMUEL

			1	2	3	4	5	6	7
8	9	10	11	12	13	14	15	16	17
18	19	20	21	22	23	24			

1 KINGS

			1	2	3	4	5	6	7
8	9	10	11	12	13	14	15	16	17
18	19	20	21	22					

2 KINGS

			1	2	3	4	5	6	7
8	9	10	11	12	13	14	15	16	17
18	19	20	21	22	23	24	25		

1 CHRONICLES

				1	2	3	4	5	6
7	8	9	10	11	12	13	14	15	16
17	18	19	20	21	22	23	24	25	26
27	28	29							

2 CHRONICLES

				1	2	3	4	5	6
7	8	9	10	11	12	13	14	15	16
17	18	19	20	21	22	23	24	25	26
27	28	29	30	31	32	33	34	35	36

EZRA

1	2	3	4	5	6	7	8	9	10

NEHEMIAH

1	2	3	4	5	6	7
8	9	10	11	12	13	

ESTHER

1	2	3	4	5	6	7	8	9	10

JOB

		1	2	3	4	5	6	7	8
9	10	11	12	13	14	15	16	17	18
19	20	21	22	23	24	25	26	27	28
29	30	31	32	33	34	35	36	37	38
39	40	41	42						

PSALMS

1	2	3	4	5	6	7	8	9	10
11	12	13	14	15	16	17	18	19	20
21	22	23	24	25	26	27	28	29	30
31	32	33	34	35	36	37	38	39	40
41	42	43	44	45	46	47	48	49	50
51	52	53	54	55	56	57	58	59	60
61	62	63	64	65	66	67	68	69	70
71	72	73	74	75	76	77	78	79	80
81	82	83	84	85	86	87	88	89	90
91	92	93	94	95	96	97	98	99	100
101	102	103	104	105	106	107	108	109	110
111	112	113	114	115	116	117	118	119	120
121	122	123	124	125	126	127	128	129	130
131	132	133	134	135	136	137	138	139	140
141	142	143	144	145	146	147	148	149	150

PROVERBS

				1	2	3	4	5	6
7	8	9	10	11	12	13	14	15	16
17	18	19	20	21	22	23	24	25	26
27	28	29	30	31					

ECCLESIASTES

				1	2	3	4	5	6
7	8	9	10	11	12				

SONG OF SOLOMON

1	2	3	4	5	6	7	8

ISAIAH

		1	2	3	4	5	6	7	8
9	10	11	12	13	14	15	16	17	18
19	20	21	22	23	24	25	26	27	28
29	30	31	32	33	34	35	36	37	38
39	40	41	42	43	44	45	46	47	48
49	50	51	52	53	54	55	56	57	58
59	60	61	62	63	64	65	66		

JEREMIAH 1 2 3 4 5 6 7 8 9 10 11 12 13 14 15 16 17 18 19 20 21 22 23 24 25 26 27 28 29 30 31 32 33 34 35 36 37 38 39 40 41 42 43 44 45 46 47 48 49 50 51 52

LAMENTATIONS 1 2 3 4 5

EZEKIEL 1 2 3 4 5 6 7 8 9 10 11 12 13 14 15 16 17 18 19 20 21 22 23 24 25 26 27 28 29 30 31 32 33 34 35 36 37 38 39 40 41 42 43 44 45 46 47 48

DANIEL 1 2 3 4 5 6 7 8 9 10 11 12

HOSEA 1 2 3 4 5 6 7 8 9 10 11 12 13 14

JOEL 1 2 3

AMOS 1 2 3 4 5 6 7 8 9

OBADIAH 1

JONAH 1 2 3 4

MICAH 1 2 3 4 5 6 7

NAHUM 1 2 3

HABAKKUK 1 2 3

ZEPHANIAH 1 2 3

HAGGAI 1 2

ZECHARIAH 1 2 3 4 5 6 7 8 9 10 11 12 13 14

MALACHI 1 2 3 4

New Testament

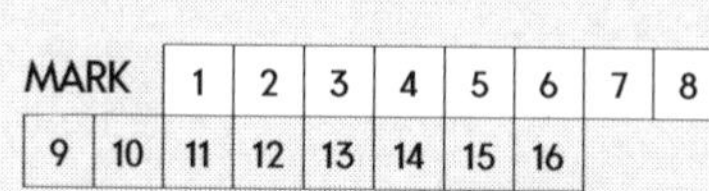

MATTHEW 1 2 3 4 5 6 7 8 9 10 11 12 13 14 15 16 17 18 19 20 21 22 23 24 25 26 27 28

MARK 1 2 3 4 5 6 7 8 9 10 11 12 13 14 15 16

LUKE 1 2 3 4 5 6 7 8 9 10 11 12 13 14 15 16 17 18 19 20 21 22 23 24

JOHN 1 2 3 4 5 6 7 8 9 10 11 12 13 14 15 16 17 18 19 20 21

ACTS 1 2 3 4 5 6 7 8 9 10 11 12 13 14 15 16 17 18 19 20 21 22 23 24 25 26 27 28

ROMANS 1 2 3 4 5 6 7 8 9 10 11 12 13 14 15 16

1 CORINTHIANS 1 2 3 4 5 6 7 8 9 10 11 12 13 14 15 16

2 CORINTHIANS 1 2 3 4 5 6 7 8 9 10 11 12 13

GALATIANS 1 2 3 4 5 6

EPHESIANS 1 2 3 4 5 6

PHILIPPIANS 1 2 3 4

COLOSSIANS 1 2 3 4

1 THESSALONIANS 1 2 3 4 5

2 THESSALONIANS 1 2 3

1 TIMOTHY 1 2 3 4 5 6

2 TIMOTHY 1 2 3 4

TITUS 1 2 3

PHILEMON 1

HEBREWS 1 2 3 4 5 6 7 8 9 10 11 12 13

JAMES 1 2 3 4 5

1 PETER 1 2 3 4 5

2 PETER 1 2 3

1 JOHN 1 2 3 4 5

2 JOHN 1

3 JOHN 1

JUDE 1

REVELATION 1 2 3 4 5 6 7 8 9 10 11 12 13 14 15 16 17 18 19 20 21 22

Month 1

Health Tracker

	1	2	3	4	5	6	7	8	9	10	11	12	13	14
Cardio														
Strength Training														
Water Intake														
Vegetables														
Fruit														
Protein														
Vitamins														
Medications														
Skin Care Routine														
Social Media < ____ min/day														

Suggestions for the Blanks: 15 minutes a day on a special project, walking the dog, no extra spending for the month, period tracker, no sugar, no carbs, no snacks, no desserts, 15-minute clean up, mood, relaxation (e.g., bubble bath, read a good book, meditate, go for a walk).

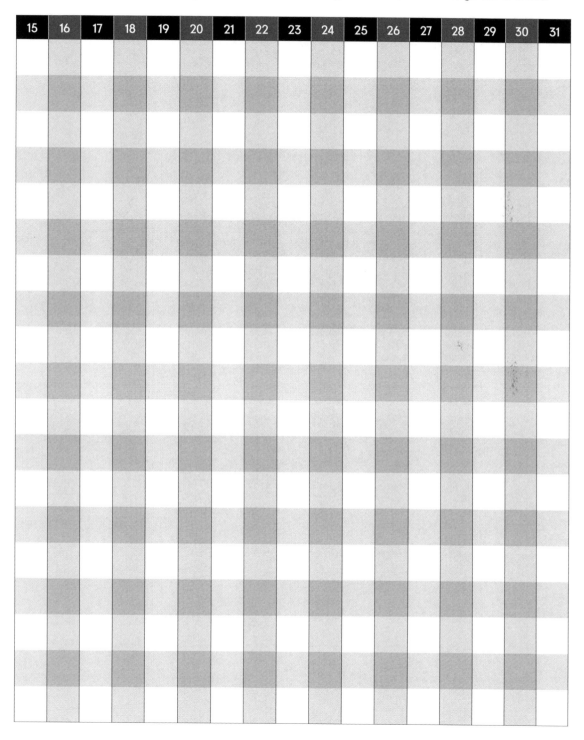

Sleep Tracker

DAY OF THE MONTH	PM			AM												PM								
	9	10	11	12	1	2	3	4	5	6	7	8	9	10	11	12	1	2	3	4	5	6	7	8
1																								
2																								
3																								
4																								
5																								
6																								
7																								
8																								
9																								
10																								
11																								
12																								
13																								
14																								
15																								
16																								
17																								
18																								
19																								
20																								
21																								
22																								
23																								
24																								
25																								
26																								
27																								
28																								
29																								
30																								
31																								

Calorie Tracker

MONTH 1

CALORIES CONSUMED

SLOW DOWN (1800–2000)

DAY OF THE MONTH	100	200	300	400	500	600	700	800	900	1000	1100	1200	1300	1400	1500	1600	1700	1800	1900	2000	
1																					STOP
2																					STOP
3																					STOP
4																					STOP
5																					STOP
6																					STOP
7																					STOP
8																					STOP
9																					STOP
10																					STOP
11																					STOP
12																					STOP
13																					STOP
14																					STOP
15																					STOP
16																					STOP
17																					STOP
18																					STOP
19																					STOP
20																					STOP
21																					STOP
22																					STOP
23																					STOP
24																					STOP
25																					STOP
26																					STOP
27																					STOP
28																					STOP
29																					STOP
30																					STOP
31																					STOP

Housework Tracker

	WEEK 1							WEEK 2							WEEK 3							WEEK 4							WEEK 5						
	S	M	T	W	T	F	S	S	M	T	W	T	F	S	S	M	T	W	T	F	S	S	M	T	W	T	F	S	S	M	T	W	T	F	S
Menu Plan																																			
Grocery Shop																																			
Wash Laundry																																			
Fold Laundry																																			
Put Away Laundry																																			
Dust																																			
Vacuum/Sweep																																			
Empty Trash Cans																																			
Clean Bathrooms																																			
Clean Kitchen																																			

	SUNDAY	MONDAY	TUESDAY	WEDNESDAY	THURSDAY	FRIDAY	SATURDAY
SUGGESTED ROUTINE	REST!	market day	tubs, toilets & towels	wash day	dust & vacuum	floor	catch-up day

	SUNDAY	MONDAY	TUESDAY	WEDNESDAY	THURSDAY	FRIDAY	SATURDAY
MY WEEKLY ROUTINE							

	SUNDAY	MONDAY	TUESDAY	WEDNESDAY	THURSDAY	FRIDAY	SATURDAY
MY WEEKLY ROUTINE							

	SUNDAY	MONDAY	TUESDAY	WEDNESDAY	THURSDAY	FRIDAY	SATURDAY
MY WEEKLY ROUTINE							

	SUNDAY	MONDAY	TUESDAY	WEDNESDAY	THURSDAY	FRIDAY	SATURDAY
MY WEEKLY ROUTINE							

Meal Planning Tracker

WEEK 1

	BREAKFAST	LUNCH	DINNER	SNACK
SUNDAY				
MONDAY				
TUESDAY				
WEDNESDAY				
THURSDAY				
FRIDAY				
SATURDAY				

Meal Planning Tracker

WEEK 2

	BREAKFAST	LUNCH	DINNER	SNACK
SUNDAY				
MONDAY				
TUESDAY				
WEDNESDAY				
THURSDAY				
FRIDAY				
SATURDAY				

Meal Planning Tracker

WEEK 3

	BREAKFAST	LUNCH	DINNER	SNACK
SUNDAY				
MONDAY				
TUESDAY				
WEDNESDAY				
THURSDAY				
FRIDAY				
SATURDAY				

Meal Planning Tracker

WEEK 4

	BREAKFAST	LUNCH	DINNER	SNACK
SUNDAY				
MONDAY				
TUESDAY				
WEDNESDAY				
THURSDAY				
FRIDAY				
SATURDAY				

Meal Planning Tracker

WEEK 5

	BREAKFAST	LUNCH	DINNER	SNACK
SUNDAY				
MONDAY				
TUESDAY				
WEDNESDAY				
THURSDAY				
FRIDAY				
SATURDAY				

Gratitude Tracker

MONTH 1

1

2

3

4

5

6

7

8

9

10

11

12

13

14

15

16

17

18

19

20

21

22

23

24

25

26	
27	
28	
29	
30	
31	

My Thoughts THIS MONTH ABOUT GRATITUDE

Notes Tracker

TITLE: SPEAKER:

Notes Tracker

TITLE: SPEAKER:

Notes Tracker

TITLE: SPEAKER:

Notes Tracker

TITLE: SPEAKER:

MONTH 1

Notes Tracker

TITLE: SPEAKER:

Month 2

Health Tracker

MONTH 2

	1	2	3	4	5	6	7	8	9	10	11	12	13	14
Cardio														
Strength Training														
Water Intake														
Vegetables														
Fruit														
Protein														
Vitamins														
Medications														
Skin Care Routine														
Social Media < ____ min/day														

Suggestions for the Blanks: 15 minutes a day on a special project, walking the dog, no extra spending for the month, period tracker, no sugar, no carbs, no snacks, no desserts, 15-minute clean up, mood, relaxation (e.g., bubble bath, read a good book, meditate, go for a walk).

15	16	17	18	19	20	21	22	23	24	25	26	27	28	29	30	31

Sleep Tracker

DAY OF THE MONTH	PM			AM												PM								
	9	10	11	12	1	2	3	4	5	6	7	8	9	10	11	12	1	2	3	4	5	6	7	8
1																								
2																								
3																								
4																								
5																								
6																								
7																								
8																								
9																								
10																								
11																								
12																								
13																								
14																								
15																								
16																								
17																								
18																								
19																								
20																								
21																								
22																								
23																								
24																								
25																								
26																								
27																								
28																								
29																								
30																								
31																								

Calorie Tracker

DAY OF THE MONTH	CALORIES CONSUMED																	SLOW DOWN			
	100	200	300	400	500	600	700	800	900	1000	1100	1200	1300	1400	1500	1600	1700	1800	1900	2000	
1																					STOP
2																					STOP
3																					STOP
4																					STOP
5																					STOP
6																					STOP
7																					STOP
8																					STOP
9																					STOP
10																					STOP
11																					STOP
12																					STOP
13																					STOP
14																					STOP
15																					STOP
16																					STOP
17																					STOP
18																					STOP
19																					STOP
20																					STOP
21																					STOP
22																					STOP
23																					STOP
24																					STOP
25																					STOP
26																					STOP
27																					STOP
28																					STOP
29																					STOP
30																					STOP
31																					STOP

Housework Tracker

	WEEK 1							WEEK 2							WEEK 3							WEEK 4							WEEK 5						
	S	M	T	W	T	F	S	S	M	T	W	T	F	S	S	M	T	W	T	F	S	S	M	T	W	T	F	S	S	M	T	W	T	F	S
Menu Plan																																			
Grocery Shop																																			
Wash Laundry																																			
Fold Laundry																																			
Put Away Laundry																																			
Dust																																			
Vacuum/Sweep																																			
Empty Trash Cans																																			
Clean Bathrooms																																			
Clean Kitchen																																			

	SUNDAY	MONDAY	TUESDAY	WEDNESDAY	THURSDAY	FRIDAY	SATURDAY
SUGGESTED ROUTINE	REST!	market day	tubs, toilets & towels	wash day	dust & vacuum	floor	catch-up day

	SUNDAY	MONDAY	TUESDAY	WEDNESDAY	THURSDAY	FRIDAY	SATURDAY
MY WEEKLY ROUTINE							

	SUNDAY	MONDAY	TUESDAY	WEDNESDAY	THURSDAY	FRIDAY	SATURDAY
MY WEEKLY ROUTINE							

	SUNDAY	MONDAY	TUESDAY	WEDNESDAY	THURSDAY	FRIDAY	SATURDAY
MY WEEKLY ROUTINE							

	SUNDAY	MONDAY	TUESDAY	WEDNESDAY	THURSDAY	FRIDAY	SATURDAY
MY WEEKLY ROUTINE							

Meal Planning Tracker

WEEK 1

	BREAKFAST	LUNCH	DINNER	SNACK
SUNDAY				
MONDAY				
TUESDAY				
WEDNESDAY				
THURSDAY				
FRIDAY				
SATURDAY				

MONTH 2

Meal Planning Tracker

WEEK 2

	BREAKFAST	LUNCH	DINNER	SNACK
SUNDAY				
MONDAY				
TUESDAY				
WEDNESDAY				
THURSDAY				
FRIDAY				
SATURDAY				

MONTH 2

Meal Planning Tracker

WEEK 3

	BREAKFAST	LUNCH	DINNER	SNACK
SUNDAY				
MONDAY				
TUESDAY				
WEDNESDAY				
THURSDAY				
FRIDAY				
SATURDAY				

Meal Planning Tracker

WEEK 4

	BREAKFAST	LUNCH	DINNER	SNACK
SUNDAY				
MONDAY				
TUESDAY				
WEDNESDAY				
THURSDAY				
FRIDAY				
SATURDAY				

MONTH 2

Meal Planning Tracker

WEEK 5

	BREAKFAST	LUNCH	DINNER	SNACK
SUNDAY				
MONDAY				
TUESDAY				
WEDNESDAY				
THURSDAY				
FRIDAY				
SATURDAY				

Gratitude Tracker

1

2

3

4

5

6

7

8

9

10

11

12

13

14

15

16

17

18

19

20

21

22

23

24

25

26	
27	
28	
29	
30	
31	

My Thoughts THIS MONTH ABOUT GRATITUDE

MONTH 2

Notes Tracker

TITLE: SPEAKER:

MONTH 2

Notes Tracker

TITLE:

SPEAKER:

MONTH 2

Notes Tracker

TITLE: SPEAKER:

Notes Tracker

TITLE: SPEAKER:

MONTH 2

Notes Tracker

TITLE: SPEAKER:

MONTH 2

Month 3

Health Tracker

	1	2	3	4	5	6	7	8	9	10	11	12	13	14
Cardio														
Strength Training														
Water Intake														
Vegetables														
Fruit														
Protein														
Vitamins														
Medications														
Skin Care Routine														
Social Media < ____ min/day														

Suggestions for the Blanks: 15 minutes a day on a special project, walking the dog, no extra spending for the month, period tracker, no sugar, no carbs, no snacks, no desserts, 15-minute clean up, mood, relaxation (e.g., bubble bath, read a good book, meditate, go for a walk).

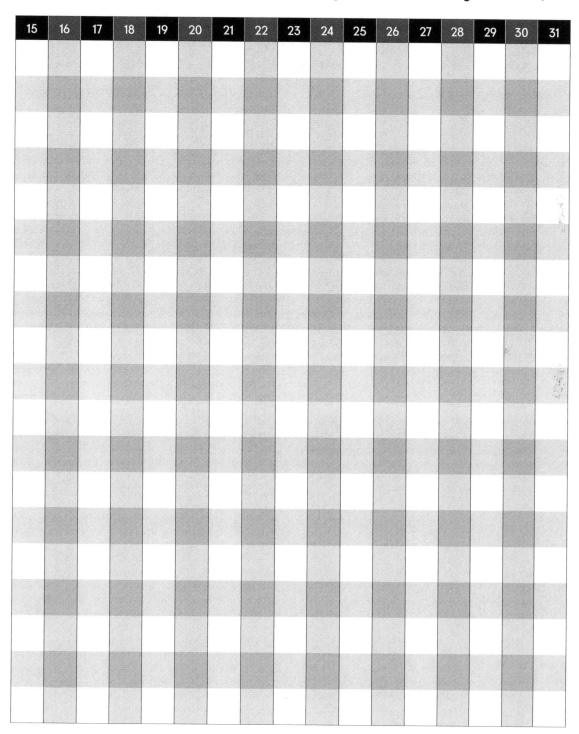

15	16	17	18	19	20	21	22	23	24	25	26	27	28	29	30	31

Sleep Tracker

	PM			AM												PM								
DAY OF THE MONTH	9	10	11	12	1	2	3	4	5	6	7	8	9	10	11	12	1	2	3	4	5	6	7	8
1																								
2																								
3																								
4																								
5																								
6																								
7																								
8																								
9																								
10																								
11																								
12																								
13																								
14																								
15																								
16																								
17																								
18																								
19																								
20																								
21																								
22																								
23																								
24																								
25																								
26																								
27																								
28																								
29																								
30																								
31																								

Calorie Tracker

CALORIES CONSUMED

DAY OF THE MONTH	100	200	300	400	500	600	700	800	900	1000	1100	1200	1300	1400	1500	1600	1700	1800 (SLOW DOWN)	1900 (SLOW DOWN)	2000 (SLOW DOWN)	
1																					STOP
2																					STOP
3																					STOP
4																					STOP
5																					STOP
6																					STOP
7																					STOP
8																					STOP
9																					STOP
10																					STOP
11																					STOP
12																					STOP
13																					STOP
14																					STOP
15																					STOP
16																					STOP
17																					STOP
18																					STOP
19																					STOP
20																					STOP
21																					STOP
22																					STOP
23																					STOP
24																					STOP
25																					STOP
26																					STOP
27																					STOP
28																					STOP
29																					STOP
30																					STOP
31																					STOP

Housework Tracker

	WEEK 1							WEEK 2							WEEK 3							WEEK 4							WEEK 5						
	S	M	T	W	T	F	S	S	M	T	W	T	F	S	S	M	T	W	T	F	S	S	M	T	W	T	F	S	S	M	T	W	T	F	S
Menu Plan																																			
Grocery Shop																																			
Wash Laundry																																			
Fold Laundry																																			
Put Away Laundry																																			
Dust																																			
Vacuum/Sweep																																			
Empty Trash Cans																																			
Clean Bathrooms																																			
Clean Kitchen																																			

	SUNDAY	MONDAY	TUESDAY	WEDNESDAY	THURSDAY	FRIDAY	SATURDAY
SUGGESTED ROUTINE	REST!	market day	tubs, toilets & towels	wash day	dust & vacuum	floor	catch-up day

	SUNDAY	MONDAY	TUESDAY	WEDNESDAY	THURSDAY	FRIDAY	SATURDAY
MY WEEKLY ROUTINE							

	SUNDAY	MONDAY	TUESDAY	WEDNESDAY	THURSDAY	FRIDAY	SATURDAY
MY WEEKLY ROUTINE							

	SUNDAY	MONDAY	TUESDAY	WEDNESDAY	THURSDAY	FRIDAY	SATURDAY
MY WEEKLY ROUTINE							

	SUNDAY	MONDAY	TUESDAY	WEDNESDAY	THURSDAY	FRIDAY	SATURDAY
MY WEEKLY ROUTINE							

Meal Planning Tracker

WEEK 1

	BREAKFAST	LUNCH	DINNER	SNACK
SUNDAY				
MONDAY				
TUESDAY				
WEDNESDAY				
THURSDAY				
FRIDAY				
SATURDAY				

Meal Planning Tracker

WEEK 2

	BREAKFAST	LUNCH	DINNER	SNACK
SUNDAY				
MONDAY				
TUESDAY				
WEDNESDAY				
THURSDAY				
FRIDAY				
SATURDAY				

Meal Planning Tracker

WEEK 3

	BREAKFAST	LUNCH	DINNER	SNACK
SUNDAY				
MONDAY				
TUESDAY				
WEDNESDAY				
THURSDAY				
FRIDAY				
SATURDAY				

MONTH 3

Meal Planning Tracker

WEEK 4

	BREAKFAST	LUNCH	DINNER	SNACK
SUNDAY				
MONDAY				
TUESDAY				
WEDNESDAY				
THURSDAY				
FRIDAY				
SATURDAY				

Meal Planning Tracker

WEEK 5

	BREAKFAST	LUNCH	DINNER	SNACK
SUNDAY				
MONDAY				
TUESDAY				
WEDNESDAY				
THURSDAY				
FRIDAY				
SATURDAY				

Gratitude Tracker

1

2

3

4

5

6

7

8

9

10

11

12

13

14

15

16

17

18

19

20

21

22

23

24

25

26	
27	
28	
29	
30	
31	

My Thoughts THIS MONTH ABOUT GRATITUDE

MONTH 3

Notes Tracker

TITLE: SPEAKER:

Notes Tracker

TITLE: SPEAKER:

MONTH 3

Notes Tracker

TITLE: SPEAKER:

Notes Tracker

TITLE: SPEAKER:

MONTH 3

Notes Tracker

TITLE: SPEAKER:

Journal

Journal

"But they who wait for the Lord shall renew their strength."

ISAIAH 40:31

Journal

"Blessed is the man who trusts in the Lord."

JEREMIAH 17:7

Journal

"Fear not, for I am with you."

ISAIAH 41:10

Journal

"The Lord is good, a stronghold in the day of trouble."

NAHUM 1:7

Journal

"Come to me, all who labor and are heavy laden."

MATTHEW 11:28

Journal

"I will give you rest."

MATTHEW 11:28

Journal

"For God so loved the world, that he gave his only Son."

JOHN 3:16

Journal

"Peace I leave with you; my peace I give to you."

JOHN 14:27

Journal

"For we walk by faith, not by sight."

2 CORINTHIANS 5:7

Journal

"If God is for us, who can be against us?"

ROMANS 8:31

Journal

"Be strong in the Lord and in the strength of his might."

EPHESIANS 6:10

Journal

"And my God will supply every need of yours."

PHILIPPIANS 4:19

Journal

"Let the peace of Christ rule in your hearts."

COLOSSIANS 3:15

Journal

"The Lord is faithful."

2 THESSALONIANS 3:3

Journal

"For the word of God is living and active."

HEBREWS 4:12

Journal

"He who promised is faithful."

HEBREWS 10:23

Journal

"I will never leave you nor forsake you."

HEBREWS 13:5

Journal

"Blessed is the man who remains steadfast under trial."

JAMES 1:12

"Draw near to God, and he will draw near to you."

JAMES 4:8

Journal

"He cares for you."

1 PETER 5:7

Journal

"He who is in you is greater than he who is in the world."

1 JOHN 4:4

Journal

"And rising very early in the morning...he prayed."

MARK 1:35

Journal

"*Joy comes with the morning.*"

PSALM 30:5

Journal

"The joy of the Lord is your strength."

NEHEMIAH 8:10

"Let all who take refuge in you rejoice."

PSALM 5:11

"The Lord is my strength and my shield."

PSALM 28:7

Journal

"Whatever you do, work heartily, as for the Lord."

COLOSSIANS 3:23

Journal

"Love your neighbor as yourself."

GALATIANS 5:14

Journal

"Whatever you do, do all to the glory of God."

1 CORINTHIANS 10:31

Journal

"It is more blessed to give than to receive."

ACTS 20:35

Journal

"Let your light shine before others."

MATTHEW 5:16

Journal

"As for me and my house, we will serve the Lord"

JOSHUA 24:15

Journal

"Unless the Lord builds the house, those who build it labor in vain."

PSALM 127:1

Journal

"Trust in the Lord with all your heart."

PROVERBS 3:5

Journal

"For by grace you have been saved through faith."

EPHESIANS 2:8

Journal

"Without faith it is impossible to please him."

HEBREWS 11:6

Journal

"Be still before the Lord and wait patiently for him."

PSALM 37:7

Journal

"Be still, and know that I am God."

PSALM 46:10

Journal

"The Lord is near to the brokenhearted."

PSALM 34:18

Journal

"*Let us not grow weary of doing good.*"

GALATIANS 6:9

Journal

"I can do all things through him who strengthens me."

PHILIPPIANS 4:13

Journal

"Be strong and courageous."

JOSHUA 1:9

Journal

"The Lord your God is with you wherever you go."

JOSHUA 1:9

Journal

"The Lord stood by me and strengthened me."

2 TIMOTHY 4:17

Journal

"In all these things we are more than conquerors through him who loved us."

ROMANS 8:37

"He has made everything beautiful in its time."

ECCLESIASTES 3:11